DEDICATED TO THE HARD WORKERS—NO MATTER WHERE OR WHEN THEY GET THE JOB DONE.

execonthedesk.com

EXEC on the DESK

the never-before-told story of how the future of work came to be

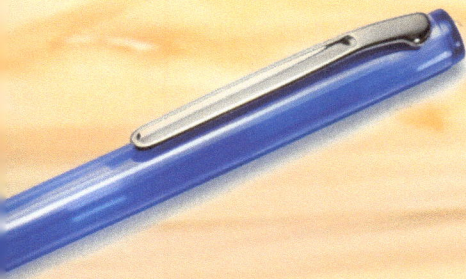

JUSTIN OWINGS

'Twas not long ago that knowledge work was cursed,
With employees all fragmented, scattered, and worse!
No agreement could be found on where to clock in,
For all could work anywhere, even the Caribbean!

But when growth started stalling, it didn't take long,
For C-suites to claim, "Remote work's all wrong!"

"Return to the office, at once, you must!
"The shared workplace is better! In the office we trust!"

COMMUTE

The workers responded, "Back to the office? Heck, no!
"There's no point in commuting with laptops in tow!"

"Cubicle or home, wherever and whenever,
"The 'net makes it easy for all to work together!"

Struggling, stagnating, and stuck in debate,
Nobody was happy, with many irate!

"If only they'd see how ridiculous they are!"
Proclaimed each side as they raged from afar.

With hope disappearing
And misery rising,
A miracle appeared,
A solution of "right" sizing.

"McKinsley's my name,
"And I see you're in trouble,
"But a workforce producing,
"I can solve on the double!"

'Twas the most magical consult,
And McKinsley held forth,
"You can guarantee productivity,
"With one true north!"

"Now, meet your new leader,
"One real micro manager!
"The Exec on the Desk,
"Your productivity enhancer!"

Curious yet confused, the bosses all asked,
"How in Jobs' name could that help our forecasts?"
With a broadening smile, McKinsley just winked,
On the big boardroom table, a helper he plinked.

BANANA
(for scale)

SIZE

— Big enough to manage anyone, anywhere
— Still small enough for carry-on luggage

SKILLS

— Tirelessly watchful
— Remembers everything
— Loyal to the company
— Scales 1:1 with your workforce
— Personalizable to the employee
— Ready to go where your people go
— Won't increase headcount (like magic!)

"By Taylor! By Ford! Your answer is here:
"You need peering eyes when workers aren't near!"

"The Exec on the Desk! They're right by their side,
"Watching and reporting, these scouts do abide!"

"Whether efficient or flailing, all's seen by wee helpers.
"Yes, everything is shared by performance tattletellers!"

"Worry no more about employee motivation,
"With millions of Execs mandating innovation!"

"Yes, the Exec on the Desk is all that you need,

"To be sure work is done anywhere," McKinsley decreed.

And just like that, the Execs got to work.

Surveilling the scene for attention that dwindles,
Execs push people harder so that no time is swindled.

As for the laptop class, they're free to roam at last,
With an Exec of their own to keep them on task.

The Exec on the Desk sees all that you do,
Vigilantly and dutifully watching over you.

Quietly resigned, the workers now muse,
"At least and at last, I can work where I choose?"

While the C-suite, managers, and investors all crow, "Our people must work harder! Let's flipping go!"

Thus ends the story of how the future of work happened.
With each worker measured and recorded, none slacken!
From CEOs to managers to smallest worker bees,
Everyone's now monitored in this distributed reality.

NOTE FROM THE AUTHOR

Work today is absurd. Leaders insist that employees drive long distances to be physically present at an office for work. They hope water coolers and hallway collisions spark innovation. Only when the people show up, the heads go down, and the headphones go on. How else do you defend yourself from the assault of the open, collision-friendly office?

Meanwhile, no matter where people go to work, all the work ends up online. Software applications make work easy and efficient from anywhere. Who needs to go to an office when you can get to work wherever and whenever you like?

Yes, remote work does have its problems. Digital media limits and distorts communication. Between the zeroes and ones, a lot gets lost. How do you get a team on the same page when, due to the dozens of apps the team uses to collaborate, no one knows with any confidence what the same page really is?

Everywhere there's the problem of trust. Large organizations have good reasons to track how often you work—or not—and on what. Software will make this tracking easier, regardless of whether it's in the office or from Tahiti. Soon, a software-powered micromanager may be a mere swipe, click, or tap away—not that you'll know it.

But the future of work need not be so dystopian, not if you can see these kinds of problems (and even laugh about them).

If you want more from work than a paycheck and a punchline, find me at ExecontheDesk.com. Together, let's imagine a future of work we can believe in—or laugh trying.

JUSTIN OWINGS

EXEC on the DESK.com

www.ingramcontent.com/pod-product-compliance
Lightning Source LLC
LaVergne TN
LVHW072135070426
835513LV00003B/109